WALKING WITH DINOSAURS
THE 3D MOVIE
DINOPEDIA

By Steve Brusatte

MACMILLAN CHILDREN'S BOOKS

Walking with Dinosaurs Dinopedia
BBC, BBC Earth and Walking with Dinosaurs are trademarks of the
British Broadcasting Corporation and are used under licence.
Walking with Dinosaurs logo © BBC 2012
BBC logo © BBC 1996
© 2013 BBC Earth MD (WWD) Limited, Evergreen MD LLC and Reliance Prodco LLC

For information address Macmillan Children's Books,
Macmillan Publisher's Limited, 20 New Wharf Road, London N1 9RR.
www.panmacmillan.com

A CIP catalogue record for this book is available from the British Library.

ISBN 978-1-4472-5158-3

Typography by Rick Farley

1 3 5 7 9 8 6 4 2

THE HISTORY OF THE EARTH AND THE GEOLOGICAL TIMESCALE

The Earth is very old, much older than the dinosaurs. The story of Earth's history began 4.54 billion years ago, when our planet was moulded out of the gas and dust left over from the formation of the Sun.

The early Earth was very different from today's world. Volcanoes erupted constantly, asteroids bombarded the planet and temperatures were so hot that most of the Earth's surface was molten lava. Over time the surface cooled down, the gases flowing out of volcanoes formed an atmosphere and rain slowly gathered into oceans. About one billion years ago, conditions were ripe for the first life forms to develop: single-celled bacteria.

The earliest plants and animals evolved probably about one billion years ago. The oldest animals were simple – sponges and jellyfish with soft bodies and only a few types

Induan 252–250 MYA	Olenekian 250–247 MYA	Anisian 247–241 MYA	Ladinian 241–237 MYA	Carnian 237–228 MYA	Norian 228–209 MYA	Rhaetian 209–201 MYA	Hettangian 201–199 MYA	Sinemurian 199–191 MYA	Pliensbachian 191–183 MYA	Toarcian 183–174 MYA	Aalenian 174–170 MYA	Bajocian 170–168 MYA	Bathonian 168–166 MYA	Callovian 166–164 MYA	Oxfordian 164–157 MYA	Kimmeridgian 157–152 MYA	Tithonian 152–145 MYA

EARLY TRIASSIC 252–247 MYA	MID-TRIASSIC 247–237 MYA	LATE TRIASSIC 237–201 MYA	EARLY JURASSIC 201–174 MYA	MID-JURASSIC 174–164 MYA	LATE JURASSIC 164–145 MYA

TRIASSIC
252–201 Million Years Ago

JURASSIC
201–145 Million Years Ago

DINOSAUR

Scientists have a standard timescale to describe the history of the Earth. The 4.54 billion years of history are divided into a series of eons, which are further divided into smaller eras, which in turn are divided into even smaller periods. The first bacteria evolved during the Proterozoic eon, but the evolution of life went into hyperdrive during the Phanerozoic eon, the time of 'visible life' that began about 540 million years ago. The Phanerozoic is divided into three eras: the Paleozoic, Mesozoic and Cenozoic. Dinosaurs flourished during the Mesozoic, which began about 250 million years ago and ended 66 million years ago. The Mesozoic is subdivided into the familiar Triassic, Jurassic and Cretaceous periods.

of cells – but larger and more complex species developed by 600 million years ago. About 150 million years later animals and plants colonized the land, creating the forests and swamplands that are so familiar today.

One of the great moments in the history of life was the evolution of vertebrates: animals with a backbone. The first vertebrates were fish that lived in the oceans, alongside trilobites and other shelled animals. Amphibians, reptiles and early relatives of mammals dominated the land during the 150 million years before the origin of the dinosaurs. But then, about 250 million years ago, the Age of Dinosaurs began.

| Berriasian 145–139 MYA | Valanginian 139–134 MYA | Hauterivian 134–131 MYA | Barremian 131–126 MYA | Aptian 126–113 MYA | Albian 113–100 MYA | Cenomanian 100–93.9 MYA | Turonian 93.9–89.8 MYA | Coniacian 89.8–86.3 MYA | Santonian 86.3–83.6 MYA | Campanian 83.6–72.1 MYA | Maastrichtian 72.1–66 MYA |

| EARLY CRETACEOUS 145–100 MYA | LATE CRETACEOUS 100–66 MYA |

CRETACEOUS
145–66 Million Years Ago

TIMESCALE

How do scientists know how old the Earth is, or when the Mesozoic started, or when the dinosaurs became extinct? They carefully study rocks using a technique called radiometric dating. Certain rocks, such as those formed in volcanoes, contain an abundance of uranium, lead and other chemical elements. Some of these elements begin to decay into other elements as soon as a rock is formed. The speed at which this occurs is also known. Therefore, by measuring the amounts of the original element and the new elements formed from decay, scientists can tell how old a rock is.

RISE OF DINOSAURS

The Age of Dinosaurs started in the aftermath of the worst period of death in Earth's history: the end-Permian extinction of 252 million years ago, during which up to ninety-five per cent of all species became extinct. So many species died out at the end of the Permian Period that entirely new groups of plants and animals had the opportunity to colonize the world during the following Triassic Period. Dinosaurs were one of these groups, as were mammals, turtles, and lizards.

There wasn't much that was special about the dinosaurs when they first evolved. Dinosaurs are a type of archosaur – a large group that also includes birds and crocodiles. The archosaurian ancestors of dinosaurs were small and fragile, no larger than a house cat and weighing just a few pounds.

Between 230–240 million years ago, the tiny, rare dinosaur ancestors gave rise to true dinosaurs. Dinosaurs are distinguished from all other animals by a few features of their skeleton. First, the hip socket – where the thigh bone fits into the pelvis – is an open hole. This would have allowed dinosaurs to walk more upright, and perhaps move faster, than other animals. Second, the upper arm bone (humerus) has a long ridge where powerful muscles attached, meaning dinosaurs had particularly strong forearms for running or grabbing prey.

For the first thirty million years of their history in the Triassic, dinosaurs weren't that impressive. They were outnumbered by their close relatives, the crocodile-like archosaurs. But many crocodile-like animals suddenly became extinct at the end of the Triassic period, about 200 million years ago, as another pulse of volcanic eruptions devastated the globe. Dinosaurs were able to survive this catastrophe and went on to become the incredible beasts that we all love.

Sterling Nesbitt's speciality is the Triassic: the period of time when dinosaurs originated and began their rise to dominance. He has discovered many new species of Triassic dinosaurs in the Western United States, and his research has shown that the rise of dinosaurs was a slow, complicated process.

HOW DO SCIENTISTS STUDY DINOSAURS?

Dinosaur palaeontologists seek to answer two major questions. First, how did dinosaurs function as living animals? Second, how did dinosaurs evolve over their 160-million-year history, a time of changing climates and moving continents? Scientists address these questions by collecting new dinosaur fossils and studying them in the lab.

The collection of new fossils is probably the most famous aspect of palaeontology. Scientists looking for new dinosaurs will try to find a place where there are rocks of the right age and right type to preserve dinosaur fossils. So this means rocks that formed on land during the Mesozoic Era. Once a suitable location is identified, the search for dinosaurs comes down to hard work and chance. Once a fossil is found it must be cleaned, protected, removed from the ground and transported back to the lab. Because many fossils are found in deserts or other areas far from cities, sometimes it takes many months to ship a fossil from the field to the lab!

Once a fossil is safe in the lab, palaeontologists use a variety of sophisticated techniques to study it and better understand what type of living, breathing animal it belonged to. Dinosaur bones are carefully measured and compared to the bones of other species. High-powered X-rays from CT scanners are commonly used to see details of the bone interior that cannot be seen by the naked eye. Bones can be cut open to reveal growth lines, which indicate how old the dinosaur was when it died. Computer models of the skeleton can be built to study how the dinosaur moved. We can even shed light on the average body temperature of the dinosaur by removing microscopic chemicals from the bone.

DINOSAUR ART

Many artists specialize in drawing, painting and sculpting dinosaurs. They are commonly referred to as palaeoartists. Their art graces the exhibit halls of museums, the pages of popular books and the internet. Sometimes they work with scientists to illustrate new fossil discoveries.

Any good palaeoartist must have both artistic skill and a firm understanding of science. Many palaeoartists are experts in dinosaur anatomy, movement and behaviour. Without knowing these things, it is very difficult to draw or sculpt a realistic dinosaur.

Many of today's top palaeoartists work with moviemakers to produce films on dinosaurs. These artists may not use traditional tools like pencils and brushes, but rather computer programs to make digital models of dinosaurs. The CGI (computer-generated imagery) used in movies like *Walking with Dinosaurs: The 3D Movie* is a prime example of this new and exciting type of 21st-century art.

Scott Hartman is an American artist who specializes in drawing dinosaur skeletons. He does careful research before drawing a skeleton, by measuring every bone of the dinosaur and checking which ways the bones fit together. He created the original drawings that were the basis for the 3D computer models of dinosaurs used in *Walking with Dinosaurs: The 3D Movie*.

David Krentz is an American animator who produces computer-generated art for movies and video games. He has animated several television documentaries and feature-length films, including *Walking with Dinosaurs: The 3D Movie*.

THE DINOSAUR FAMILY TREE

One of the major goals of dinosaur research is to construct the family tree of dinosaurs. The technical term for a family tree is a *cladogram*. A cladogram shows how various species of dinosaurs are related to one another. Similarly, a cladogram tells the story of the evolutionary history of dinosaurs, from their origin as small creatures 230 million years ago until their extinction.

Researchers build family trees by studying the skeletons of dinosaurs. By comparing the bones of many dinosaur species, scientists can recognize certain features that some, but not all, species share. For instance, some dinosaurs may possess claws but others do not. Because organisms share characteristics as the result of evolution, it is most likely that those species that possess a certain feature are more closely related to each other than to species that lack that feature.

The cladogram here shows how the major groups of dinosaurs are related to one another. It shows that dinosaurs are divided into two main subgroups: the saurischians (in which the front bone of the hip points forward) and the ornithischians (in which the front bone of the hip points backwards). Each of these groups is subdivided into ever more specific groups.

It is important to remember that a cladogram shows a relative pattern of relationships. For example, *Tyrannosaurus* is not the ancestor of *Velociraptor*, but rather these two predators are more closely related to each other than either one is to other dinosaurs (such as the long-necked sauropods or armoured stegosaurs).

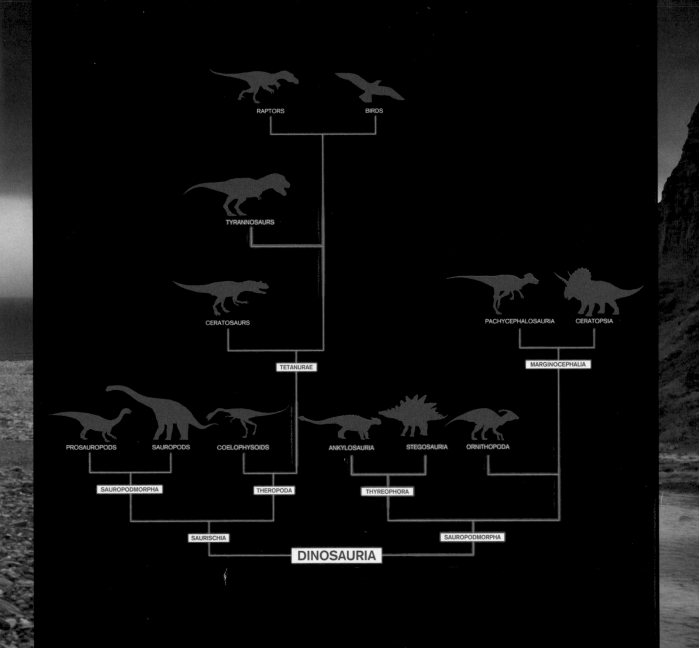

RAPTORS · BIRDS

TYRANNOSAURS

CERATOSAURS

PACHYCEPHALOSAURIA · CERATOPSIA

TETANURAE

MARGINOCEPHALIA

PROSAUROPODS · SAUROPODS · COELOPHYSOIDS · ANKYLOSAURIA · STEGOSAURIA · ORNITHOPODA

SAUROPODMORPHA · THEROPODA · THYREOPHORA

SAURISCHIA · SAUROPODMORPHA

DINOSAURIA

Roger Benson is a British palaeontologist who teaches at Oxford University. Much of his research focuses on building the family tree for the meat-eating dinosaurs (the theropods).

13

DRIFTING CONTINENTS

The Earth is always changing. The animals and plants that are alive today have not always been around. The climate we are used to is different from the climate the dinosaurs would have experienced. Not even the land we live on is stable. The seven continents of today's world have not always been in the same position. They have moved around over time. The understanding that continents move was one of the great discoveries of 20th-century science. This idea is called continental drift.

Continents move because the surface of the Earth is divided into several segments called plates. These plates slide against one another, creating earthquakes. They also move apart from each other in some places, forming oceans between them, and collide together in other places, creating mountains.

Dinosaurs lived on continents that were very different from our own. The first dinosaurs lived on the supercontinent Pangaea: a single landmass created when many smaller continents merged together. Pangaea began to break apart about 200 million years ago, as the Atlantic Ocean formed between North America and Europe. The intense volcanic eruptions that accompanied this violent split may have caused the great extinction at the end of the Triassic Period. During the next 100 million years the continents continued to split and move. By the end of the Age of Dinosaurs, some 66 million years ago, the continents basically were located in the same places they are today.

Paul Upchurch is a British palaeontologist who works in London. He is interested in how the movement of continents affected the evolution of dinosaurs. Paul's research has shown that many early dinosaur groups lived all around the world, probably because it was easy to move around on a single supercontinent.

Movement of the plates is driven by intense heat in the interior of the Earth. Sometimes this heat escapes to the surface through volcanoes.

PANGAEA

EURASIA

NORTH AMERICA

AFRICA

SOUTH AMERICA

INDIA

ANTARCTICA

AUSTRALIA

THE CRETACEOUS WORLD

The Cretaceous Period – the final flourishing of the Age of Dinosaurs – was dramatically different from today. Cretaceous dinosaurs like *Tyrannosaurus*, *Gorgosaurus*, *Pachyrhinosaurus* and *Troodon* lived in a hothouse world, in which temperatures were much higher than they are now. This extreme weather was probably a result of volcanoes.

Little or no water was locked up in the polar regions as ice or glaciers, so during much of the Cretaceous Period, shallow seas stretched all the way from the Gulf of Mexico to the Arctic Ocean, across the entire central part of North America.

Something critical happened during the Cretaceous Period: the first flowering plants evolved. Flowering plants, technically known as angiosperms, are all of those plants with flowers and fruits. In today's world these include everything from grasses and oaks to palms, sunflowers and cacti. Not all of these groups were around during the Cretaceous, but by the end of the period large trees such as magnolias were common, and the first grasses were spreading around the world. Meanwhile, other types of plants such as gymnosperms (the 'evergreen' trees) and ferns were still diverse and provided a steady food source for plant-eating dinosaurs.

The Cretaceous was a time of intense volcanic eruptions, and the carbon dioxide belched out during these explosions would have heated the planet. Something similar is happening today, as our planet is rapidly warming because of the carbon dioxide produced by burning oil and coal.

WHAT ELSE LIVED WITH DINOSAURS?

Although the Mesozoic Era is often called the Age of Dinosaurs, dinosaurs were not the only animals that thrived during this time. Living alongside the dinosaurs on land was a range of crocodiles, lizards, snakes, mammals and pterosaurs. The oldest mammals evolved in the Triassic along with the dinosaurs, but throughout the Mesozoic they rarely reached sizes larger than a fox.

Mesozoic crocodiles were much more diverse than their modern-day descendants, which we know as slow-moving sprawlers. They included fast runners, plant eaters, and even fully ocean-living species!

The Mesozoic oceans were teeming with life. The top predators in Mesozoic oceans and seas were mostly reptiles. The long-necked plesiosaurs prospered during much of the Jurassic and Cretaceous Periods. They used their paddles to fly through the water, and some species reached huge sizes, maybe even larger than *Tyrannosaurus rex*. During the latest Cretaceous, when warm seas covered much of the continents and plesiosaurs were in decline, another group of fierce predatory reptiles evolved: the mosasaurs. Meanwhile, throughout much of the Mesozoic, dolphin-like ichthyosaurs lived across the globe. These fast-swimming reptiles probably ate mostly shellfish and other smaller creatures, but some might have been top predators as well.

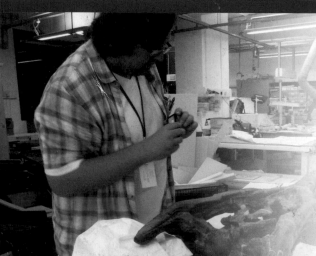

Mark Young is a Scottish palaeontologist. He is fascinated by the metriorhynchids, a bizarre group of ocean-dwelling crocodiles that lived worldwide during much of the Jurassic and Cretaceous Periods.

THE DINOSAUR-BIRD EVOLUTIONARY TRANSITION

We all know that dinosaurs are extinct. Or are they? As it turns out, not all dinosaurs are dead. That's because living birds are the evolutionary descendants of dinosaurs. Birds evolved from small, carnivorous theropod dinosaurs. So if we are to be completely accurate, birds *are* dinosaurs, in the same way that humans are mammals. And that means dinosaurs still live today.

The idea that birds evolved from dinosaurs is probably the single most important fact ever discovered by dinosaur palaeontologists.

Scientists first noted the amazing similarity between dinosaurs and birds in the 1860s, when a fossil of the oldest known bird was discovered in Germany. This 150-million-year-old bird, which was called *Archaeopteryx*, was covered in a coat of feathers and had a wishbone, both characteristic features of birds that are not known in any other living animal. But it also had teeth and a long tail, neither of which is seen in any living bird. *Archaeopteryx*, therefore, seems to have been a mixture of dinosaur and bird!

But the most remarkable discoveries did not come to light until the 1990s. Deep in the farmlands of northeastern China, villagers began to find strange fossil bones surrounded by feather impressions. These were true dinosaurs – animals very closely related to *Velociraptor* and *Tyrannosaurus*. Today, the 'feathered dinosaurs' of China are the most beautiful and visual proof that birds evolved from dinosaurs. This idea is no longer seriously debated among scientists. It has become scientific fact.

Living birds share hundreds of features of the skeleton with dinosaurs, including things like wishbones, a wrist that can fold against the body (to protect the wing) and hollow bones, which are filled with extensions of the lung called air sacs. There is behavioral evidence as well. Amazing dinosaur fossils have been found on top of nests, protecting their eggs in the same style as living birds. And the evidence goes on and on. So when you look out at a flock of geese, or a pigeon strutting around town, you are actually looking at a dinosaur!

WARM-BLOODED DINOSAURS?

It used to be thought that dinosaurs were something like overgrown lizards. They had scaly skin, moved slowly, had a cool body temperature and grew at a slow pace. But new research clearly shows that these ideas are incorrect. Dinosaurs were active animals, full of energy and capable of moving fast. They were much more like living birds and mammals than crocodiles or lizards.

In the 1970s, the discovery of new fossils, such as the small carnivore *Deinonychus*, revealed that some dinosaurs had very birdlike skeletons. This led scientists to ask whether they may have shared other features with birds as well.

This began a forty-year period in which scientists actively debated whether dinosaurs were 'warm-blooded' or 'cold-blooded'. Warm-blooded animals, like birds and mammals, control their body temperature internally. This lifestyle requires a lot of energy, so mammals and birds must eat a huge amount of food, but it also enables them to grow quickly, move fast, and lead active lifestyles. Cold-blooded animals, like crocodiles and lizards, are very different. Their body temperature relies on the temperature of the outside environment. They cannot easily live in cold climates, and usually grow much more slowly and lead much less dynamic lifestyles than warm-blooded animals.

So were dinosaurs warm-blooded or cold-blooded? This question is difficult to answer because we cannot measure the temperature of dinosaurs directly. But most evidence clearly points in one direction: dinosaurs were active, energetic creatures that grew fast. Studies of bone texture tell us that dinosaurs grew from embryos into adults quite quickly. Dinosaurs had air sacs extending from their lungs into their bones, much like birds. The feathers of many dinosaurs would have been useful in keeping the animal warm, by preventing body heat from escaping into the environment. These are some of the lines of evidence supporting an active, athletic, and maybe even warm-blooded lifestyle for dinosaurs.

Robert Eagle and Aradhna Tripati are geologists who work in Los Angeles, California. Along with colleagues, they realized that by studying the chemistry of teeth they could work out the body temperature of an animal.

DINOSAUR EGGS AND BABIES

All dinosaur species laid eggs. Some are spherical like a ball, others are more oval shaped and some have a tapered end like a chicken egg. But no matter what shape, no known dinosaur egg is larger than about the size of a football. This means that all dinosaurs, even the mightiest species like *Tyrannosaurus* and *Brachiosaurus*, were tiny when they hatched.

Some nests are little more than a random jumble of eggs set within a hole that the mother dug in the ground. Most nests of the long-necked sauropods are like this. But the birdlike theropods, on the other hand, built more ordered nests in which the eggs are gathered into a circle. Some of these nests have been found surrounded with rims of dirt, probably used as a barrier to keep predators away. Others have raised platforms that the mother or father could have sat on while guarding the eggs.

Some dinosaur species had vast nesting grounds that parents would return to year after year to lay eggs and begin raising their families. We know this because, in a few exceptional cases, huge numbers of nests are found together, spread out over hundreds of square miles. One of the most famous of these is a site in Argentina called Auca Mahuevo, which contains thousands of sauropod eggs.

Darla Zelenitsky is a Canadian palaeontologist who is one of the world's experts on dinosaur eggs. She has studied the evolution of birdlike eggs and parenting traits.

HOW DID DINOSAURS GROW?

How did some dinosaurs like *Tyrannosaurus* and *Diplodocus* become so big? Many years ago, scientists viewed dinosaurs as cold-blooded and lazy creatures. It was thought that huge dinosaurs achieved their large size by growing very slowly but living a very long time, maybe even over a hundred years.

But like so many older ideas about dinosaurs, this turns out not to be true. Dinosaurs actually grew very quickly from a tiny hatchling into a full-bodied adult. Small dinosaurs, such as *Troodon* and *Velociraptor*, would have reached full size in just a few years at most. Much larger species such as *Tyrannosaurus* would have taken longer to grow into adult size, but probably no more than about twenty years. Even the most colossal dinosaurs of all, the long-necked sauropods, probably didn't live to be much older than fifty or sixty years old, and grew to their full size long before this time.

The secrets of dinosaur growth are locked away deep inside their bones. If you cut open a dinosaur bone, take a very thin slice and look at it under a microscope, you can see growth rings. These are just like the rings in a tree trunk. One ring is formed every year during the winter months when the bone stops growing because food is scarce. This means that you can tell the age of a dinosaur fossil by counting the number of growth rings!

Scientists have counted rings of many dinosaurs. These rings are widely separated from each other deep inside the bone, meaning dinosaurs grew fast when they were young. But they are closer together toward the edges of the bone, showing that growth slowed as full size was reached. To date, scientists haven't counted anything close to a hundred growth rings, meaning it is unlikely that dinosaurs lived to a century.

Gregory Erickson is a palaeontologist and biologist at Florida State University in the United States. He is an expert on dinosaur growth. Greg has cut open many dinosaur bones to count growth lines. It was his research that showed how *Tyrannosaurus* reached huge size by growing rapidly during its teenage years.

DINOSAUR HERDS

Some dinosaurs were social creatures that gathered together in herds, packs and other groups. Scientists know that some dinosaurs formed social groups because of two very different types of fossil evidence.

First, palaeontologists have discovered several dinosaur bone beds. These are huge fossil sites where the skeletons of many dinosaurs of the same species are jumbled together. The Late Cretaceous horned ceratopsids and duck-billed hadrosaurids are commonly found in bone beds. Even the large carnivorous tyrannosaurs *Albertosaurus* and *Tarbosaurus* have been found in smaller bone beds, containing about ten skeletons. The fact that these dinosaurs are found in bone beds is strong evidence that they lived and died together. Ceratopsids and hadrosaurids probably formed huge herds that may have even migrated during the winter. Tyrannosaurs probably formed smaller hunting packs.

The second line of evidence comes from footprints. Sometimes tens of thousands of dinosaur footprints are found together at so-called megatracksites. These footprints mostly belong to the same species and are all facing in the same direction. This is strong evidence that these sites were formed by hundreds or thousands of members of a herd, travelling together and at about the same speed. The footprints of long-necked sauropods have been found in megatracksites, indicating that these dinosaurs herded together. Megatracksites are also known for some plant-eating ornithopod dinosaurs.

Joshua Mathews is an American palaeontologist. He was a student on a field trip in Montana when a volunteer discovered the first ever example of multiple *Triceratops* skeletons found together. Josh conducted a student research project on this site and argued that the *Triceratops* individuals were members of a herd.

POLAR DINOSAURS

Dinosaurs lived all across the world and in many environments. Their fossils have been found on all continents, even Antarctica. Of course, not every dinosaur species ranged across the entire planet. Different dinosaurs were adapted for living in different places.

One of the most interesting discoveries of the past few decades is that many dinosaurs lived in the cold and dark polar regions, at the very top and bottom of the Earth. Climates were warmer during the Age of Dinosaurs than they are today. There were probably no glaciers during this period, but the North and South poles would still have been quite cold. And they would have been very dark during most of the winter and light during much of the summer, just like today.

Fossils of polar dinosaurs have been found in Cretaceous rocks in Alaska and Australia. The dinosaurs that lived in these areas were common and diverse. They include the usual types of dinosaurs found in warmer areas during the Cretaceous: carnivorous theropods, horned ceratopsians and plant-eating ornithopods.

Anthony Fiorillo is an American palaeontologist who works in Dallas, Texas. For many years he has searched for dinosaurs in the cold polar state of Alaska. Tony recently discovered a new species of the horned dinosaur *Pachyrhinosaurus* that lived only in Alaska. He consulted on *Walking with Dinosaurs: The 3D Movie* by providing a wealth of information on the Alaskan dinosaurs he knows so well.

PACHYRHINOSAURUS

Pachyrhinosaurus was just one of many species of ceratopsids – the horned and frilled dinosaurs – that lived in North America during the latest Cretaceous, the final few million years of the Age of Dinosaurs. A close cousin of *Pachyrhinosaurus* is *Triceratops*, one of the most famous dinosaurs. Like *Triceratops*, *Pachyrhinosaurus* was a large plant eater that walked on four legs and had a huge skull with horns. It was something like a dinosaur version of a bull.

Pachyrhinosaurus was a large dinosaur, but nowhere near the size of *Tyrannosaurus* or the sauropods. An average adult was between 20–26 feet in length, about 5–7 feet tall at the hips, and weighed between 2–4 tons. It was about average in size for a ceratopsid. *Triceratops* was a bit bigger, but other cousins were smaller. *Pachyrhinosaurus* lived from about 74–69 million years ago, a few million years before *Triceratops*.

The first fossils of *Pachyrhinosaurus* were discovered in 1946 in Alberta, Canada, by the legendary fossil hunter Charles M. Sternberg. Later scientists continued to find new skeletons of *Pachyrhinosaurus*. Today three distinct species are recognized, including one that lived only in the cold and dark polar regions of Alaska.

The most distinctive feature of *Pachyrhinosaurus* is its elaborate skull, which was covered in horns and bumps of many different sizes and shapes. All ceratopsids had a long snout at the front of the skull and a huge, thin, plate-like frill at the back. Most species also had some type of horns. But the details of the horns were different in each species. *Triceratops* had three large horns: one over each eye and one above the nose.

Andrew Farke is a scientist working in California. He has built computer models to study the frills of ceratopsids. These models show that the frills were actually quite strong, even though they were really thin.

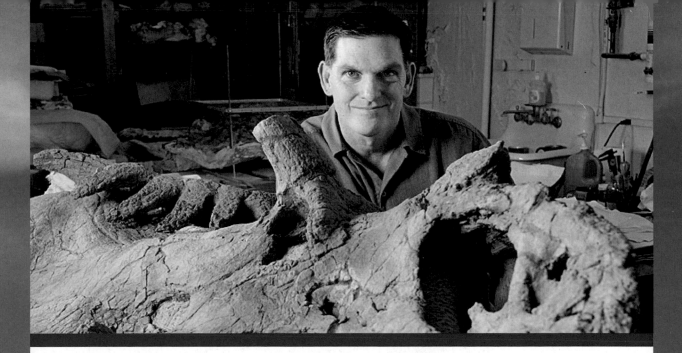

Scott Sampson is an American palaeontologist and television personality who consulted on *Walking with Dinosaurs: The 3D Movie* by providing information on the appearance, behaviour, and movement of the dinosaurs. Scott specializes in the study of the horned ceratopsid dinosaurs.

Lawrence Witmer is a specialist on dinosaur anatomy – the shapes, sizes and other details of their skeletons. He often uses sophisticated equipment like CT scanners to study dinosaur skulls. He scanned a *Pachyrhinosaurus* skull and showed that its brain was small and poorly developed, meaning that it probably wasn't a very intelligent animal.

This was not the case in *Pachyrhinosaurus*. Instead, the parts of the skull above the eyes and nose were covered with a mass of thick, rough bone. These are called 'cranial bosses'. They are basically huge bumps, and they probably would have been covered with keratin, the same material that makes up our fingernails. *Pachyrhinosaurus* also had a few horns, but these were smaller than those of *Triceratops* and located far back on the skull, on the frill.

The horns and bosses of ceratopsids were not usually present on the skulls of young individuals and appeared during the teenage years. The fact that the horns and bosses show up when the animal was going through puberty and getting ready to mate is good evidence that they were used to attract the attention of mates, or to scare off potential rivals who might want to fight over a mate. They also could have been used to push around rivals during such fights, just as male bison today will often charge one another and lock horns to compete for a mate.

Pachyrhinosaurus was a herbivore – an animal that ate only plants. Because it walked on four legs and didn't have a long neck, it would have fed on small bushes and shrubs growing on the ground. Ceratopsids like *Pachyrhinosaurus* were well adapted for eating plants. They had hundreds of small teeth in their jaws, which were packed tightly together so that each jaw had a long, sharp row of teeth. When the upper and lower jaws came together these rows would have sheared past each other like a pair of scissors. The packed tooth rows are called

John Scannella is a graduate student at Montana State University in the United States. He studies how the skull of *Triceratops* changed as it grew from a hatchling into an adult. Most interestingly, *Triceratops* developed larger and fancier horns as it got older. This is important evidence that the horns were mostly used to attract mates, not defend against predators.

'dental batteries'. They would have allowed ceratopsids to eat tough plants like evergreen leaves. They also would have allowed animals like *Pachyrhinosaurus* to quickly chop up a large amount of plant matter before swallowing. This was important because ceratopsids were big animals and needed to eat a lot of food to stay active.

One of the most amazing facts about *Pachyrhinosaurus* is that it formed large herds, much like bison and gazelles do today. Scientists know this because hundreds of *Pachyrhinosaurus* skeletons have been found together in fossil bone beds. One bone bed at Pipestone Creek in Alberta is so large that thousands of bones have already been discovered there. About a hundred bones are packed into each square metre of rock! Scientists have been digging up this bone bed for nearly thirty years and are still finding new skeletons. These include the skeletons of juveniles and adults, which show that *Pachyrhinosaurus* herds included individuals of all ages and sizes. It is likely that these herds migrated north and south, depending on the season.

GORGOSAURUS

No dinosaur is more famous or feared than *Tyrannosaurus rex*. *T. rex* was truly the king of dinosaurs: a 42 foot-long, 5-ton superpredator that could eat what it wanted, when it wanted. *T. rex* lived right at the end of the Age of Dinosaurs, about 67–66 million years ago, in North America. But a few million years earlier, several close cousins of *T. rex* lived across much of North America. One of these was *Gorgosaurus*.

Gorgosaurus was a ferocious dinosaur that ate meat and walked on two legs, just like its famous cousin. But *Gorgosaurus* was a bit smaller than *T. rex*. A full-grown adult was about 26–30 feet long and weighed around 2 tons. It was also more slender than *T. rex*, with longer legs and the ability to run faster. Fossils of *Gorgosaurus* are commonly found in the Canadian province of Alberta and the American state of Montana. It would have lived about 77–74 million years ago, making it one of the first large tyrannosaurs to dominate the North American scene.

Gorgosaurus was a classic tyrannosaur. It had all of the familiar features of the group: a big skull, thick teeth, a long tail and puny arms that were no bigger than the arms of a human! Scientists still debate what these arms could have been used for. *Gorgosaurus* was no weight lifter, that's for sure. But the arms must have been used for something, because although they are small they are still quite strong and capable of a wide range of motion.

Thomas Carr is a Canadian palaeontologist working in the United States. He is one of the world's experts on tyrannosaurs. His work has shown that the skulls of tyrannosaurs became much larger, deeper, and stronger as a juvenile changed into an adult.

Tyrannosaurs like *Gorgosaurus* were apex predators – they were at the top of the food chain and didn't have to worry about competition from smaller meat eaters. The skeleton of tyrannosaurs was well adapted for their carnivorous lifestyle. The huge skull boasted up to 70 thick, banana-sized teeth. Massive muscles powered the jaws. Some of the bones of the snout were fused together to give them extra strength. All together, these features allowed tyrannosaurs to eat essentially whatever they wanted.

But tyrannosaurs could do more than just kill and eat their prey. They also did something truly bizarre: they crunched bone as they fed. Bite marks matching the size and shape of tyrannosaur teeth are known from several ceratopsid and hadrosaurid bones. These are not shallow scratches, but rather deep pits. So tyrannosaurs must have crunched right through the bones of their prey! This is confirmed by a study of tyrannosaur coprolites – fossilized dung – that are full of bone chunks. Bone crunching sets tyrannosaurs apart from most other animals, as this behaviour is not known in other predatory dinosaurs or living reptiles.

Tyrannosaurs like *Gorgosaurus* probably lived and hunted in packs, at least some of the time. Several skeletons of the same species have been found together in bone beds. Both juveniles and adults are found together, suggesting that tyrannosaurs of many ages lived side by side, and maybe even hunted together.

John Hutchinson is an American biologist and palaeontologist who works in London. He studies dinosaur locomotion: how dinosaurs moved. John and his colleagues built a set of computer models to study how *T. rex* moved and how fast it could run. These models clearly showed that *T. rex* was not a speed demon, but rather that its huge size could only move at a much slower pace.

Thomas Holtz is an expert on the carnivorous dinosaurs, their family tree and their feeding habits. He consulted on *Walking with Dinosaurs: The 3D Movie* by providing information on the skeletons of dinosaurs and the storyline of the film.

One thing that tyrannosaurs could not do was run very fast, at least as adults. Scientists have built computer models of tyrannosaur skeletons to estimate how fast they could run. *T. rex* probably couldn't move faster than about 11–25 miles per hour. This is considerably faster than most humans (the fastest a human has ever run is Usain Bolt's 28 miles per hour during the 100-metre race), and probably faster than *Triceratops* and other potential prey.

Juvenile and adult tyrannosaurs had some features that were very different from each other. Of course, as is usual, adults were much larger than juveniles. But the differences went further than this. Juveniles had longer legs and more slender skeletons, suggesting that they could run much faster than the heavier, stockier adults. The skulls of juveniles didn't have the thick teeth and huge muscles of adults, so they couldn't bite as hard. Although they still ate meat, juveniles almost certainly couldn't crunch through bone like adults could. Instead of relying on a huge and powerful skull to capture and tear up prey, juveniles probably used their hands and claws. The arms of juveniles were much larger and stronger (relative to their size) than the arms of adults. Their hands were capped with sharp claws that could rip open prey. So adult tyrannosaurs probably relied more on strength, whereas juveniles depended more on speed.

Gorgosaurus and *T. rex* are some of the largest and last surviving tyrannosaurs. Not all tyrannosaurs were so big, nor did they all live at the end of the Cretaceous Period. The tyrannosaur group evolved more than 100 million years before *T. rex*. The earliest tyrannosaurs like *Dilong*, *Guanlong* and *Proceratosaurus* were human-sized animals that could run fast, but which lived in the shadow of other giant dinosaur predators like *Allosaurus* and *Spinosaurus*. Some of these early tyrannosaurs have even been found covered in feathers! This makes it most likely that *T. rex* and *Gorgosaurus* also would have had some sort of feathers on their body. Maybe they weren't fully feathered like a bird, but had a reduced coat of feathers much like an elephant has a thin coat of hair.

Gabe Bever studies dinosaur anatomy and growth in his laboratory in New York. Gabe led a team that described the brain of *Alioramus*, a long-snouted tyrannosaur from Asia that is a close relative of *T. rex* and *Gorgosaurus*. Tyrannosaurs like *Alioramus* had large brains and could hear a wide range of sounds. They were clearly intelligent dinosaurs that used their senses to hunt prey.

CHIROSTENOTES

Oviraptorosaurs are some of the most bizarre dinosaurs to ever live. They looked more like aliens out of a bad science fiction movie than an actual living, breathing type of animal. They were theropods – members of that great group of carnivorous dinosaurs that includes *Tyrannosaurus* and *Velociraptor* – but they probably didn't eat meat all of the time. Most species had no teeth, but their jaws were covered with a sharp beak like that of a bird. Some species had wacky crests of bone on the top of their skulls. Most oviraptorosaurs were probably covered in feathers, and some even had a big fan of feathers at the end of their tail, like a peacock.

Chirostenotes is one of the best known oviraptorosaurs. It lived in North America during the final 10–12 million years of the Cretaceous Period, alongside *Tyrannosaurus*, *Triceratops* and many other iconic dinosaurs. It was one of the smaller dinosaurs in its ecosystem. Most individuals were about 5–7 feet long from head to tail and 3–7 feet tall at the hips. While it is difficult to estimate exactly, it's unlikely that they weighed much. Many bones of their skeleton were hollowed out and filled with air sacs, which would have reduced the weight of the animal.

Several fragmentary fossils of *Chirostenotes* have been found in western Canada and the United States, but most of these consist of only a few bones.

The currently known fossils tell us that *Chirostenotes* had long legs well suited for running and huge arms that ended in large, pointed claws. The claws might have been used to capture prey, or perhaps for defence. There is still much debate about what *Chirostenotes* and its relatives ate. They certainly didn't eat meat in the same style that *Tyrannosaurus* and *Velociraptor* did, because they didn't have any teeth to cut or slice their prey. They might have eaten smaller mammals and lizards, or perhaps their strong skulls and beaks were adapted for eating hard foods like nuts or eggs.

Amy Balanoff is a scientist who works in New York. Amy studied nearly every oviraptorosaur fossil that had ever been found and built a family tree for these animals by grouping together species that share features of the skeleton. She also studied the brains of oviraptorosaurs and other birdlike dinosaurs to better understand how some classic features of the bird brain evolved.

Mark Norell is the curator of dinosaurs at the world-famous American Museum of Natural History in New York. He has hunted for dinosaurs in Mongolia's Gobi Desert for over twenty years. Mark and his team have discovered many important oviraptorosaur fossils, including the skeletons of parents sitting on their nests!

Several fragmentary fossils of *Chirostenotes* have been found in western Canada and the United States, but most of these are only a few bones. A spectacular skeleton was recently discovered but is still awaiting study by scientists. This is something to look forward to. When this skeleton is finally studied it promises to tell us more about oviraptorosaurs than we ever knew before.

TROODON

The small, fast, smart dinosaur *Troodon* is one of the closest relatives of birds. It probably looked quite a bit like a bird, and behaved like a bird as well. *Troodon* wasn't big or strong, and it may have blended into the North American Cretaceous landscape that was dominated by *T. rex*. But it was a very interesting dinosaur that had an unusual diet and a remarkably high level of intelligence.

Troodon is one of several dinosaurs classified together into a larger group called Troodontidae. Other troodontids include *Saurornithoides*, *Zanabazar* and *Sinovenator*. These are some of the rarest dinosaur fossils of all. Their skeletons have been found in Late Cretaceous rocks in North America and Asia, but not many other places. *Troodon* itself lived during the final twelve million years of the Cretaceous Period and ranged across North America, all the way up to the polar highlands of Alaska.

Philip Currie is a renowned palaeontologist and professor at the University of Alberta in Canada. He is particularly interested in dinosaurs like *Troodon*. He studies these animals to better understand how birds evolved. Phil consulted on *Walking with Dinosaurs: The 3D Movie* by providing information on dinosaur migration.

Rui Pei is a Chinese student who studies dinosaurs. He is working on his PhD at Columbia University in New York and works at the American Museum of Natural History. Rui's research focuses on the troodontid dinosaurs – the group including *Troodon* and its closest relatives.

Troodontids were close relatives of the dromaeosaurids, the familiar group of small, fierce theropods like *Velociraptor* and *Deinonychus*. The size, skeletons and behaviour of troodontids and dromaeosaurids were very similar. Members of both groups were adapted for speed, as they had light skeletons with long legs. Both groups had a large, sharp, sickle-shaped claw on each foot. And both had long-snouted skulls with large eyes and a huge brain.

Troodon itself has the largest brain relative to its body size of any dinosaur that has ever been studied. Its brain was about the size of a tennis ball, which is pretty large for a dog-sized dinosaur. In comparison, the huge long-necked sauropods had much smaller brains, only about the size of a walnut. Compared to these sauropods, as well as most other dinosaurs, *Troodon* was a genius.

The diet of *Troodon* has been the subject of much debate among scientists. The speed-adapted skeleton, large eyes and brain, and deadly foot claws all suggest that *Troodon* was a meat eater. But the story may not be so simple. The teeth of *Troodon* are very unusual for a carnivore. They are not the thin, knifelike teeth with tiny serrations that are commonly seen in *Velociraptor*, *Allosaurus* and most dinosaur predators. Instead, *Troodon* teeth are thick and have large serrations – called denticles – lining the front and back edges. These features are more common in plant-eating dinosaurs and reptiles. It is likely that *Troodon* was able to eat both meat and plants. This type of animal is known as an omnivore.

HESPERONYCHUS

Hesperonychus is one of the newest dinosaurs known to science. It was discovered in 2009, buried in a jumble of small dinosaur bones that had been collected in the Late Cretaceous rocks of Canada more than twenty-five years earlier. But although it is new, *Hesperonychus* is very important for two main reasons. First, it is one of the smallest dinosaurs ever found. Second, it is one of the closest relatives to birds, and may help scientists better understand how birds evolved.

Hesperonychus is a dromaeosaurid – a member of the group of small, fast, meat-eating dinosaurs including *Velociraptor*, *Deinonychus*, *Microraptor* and *Rahonavis*. Most dromaeosaurids range from about the size of a human down to the size of a poodle. But *Hesperonychus* was much smaller: it was probably only 1–2 feet long from head to tail and weighed as little as 2–4 pounds.

Very little is known about the diet and lifestyle of *Hesperonychus*. This is because only a few of its bones have ever been found. These bones are enough to show that *Hesperonychus* was a close relative of *Velociraptor* and *Deinonychus*. This also probably means that it was a fast runner and ate meat, just like its relatives. But scientists cannot be certain until more fossils of *Hesperonychus* are discovered.

Nicholas Longrich: As a graduate student Nick discovered the bones of *Hesperonychus* in a museum collection. In 2009 he and his advisor, Philip Currie, joined together to name this new dinosaur.

Mátyás Vremir is a geologist, caver, and adventurer who lives in Romania. In 2009 Mátyás discovered the skeleton of a small, fast dinosaur that looks very similar to *Velociraptor*, but with one main difference: it has two huge, sickle-shaped claws on each foot instead of one! Mátyás, another Romanian palaeontologist named Zoltán Csiki, and their colleagues named this new dinosaur *Balaur bondoc* in 2010.

Dromaeosaurids are some of the closest cousins to birds. *Hesperonychus* itself appears to be one of the closest relatives of the peculiar dromaeosaurid *Microraptor*. *Microraptor* is known from several specimens found in China. Both the arms and legs sport a full array of feathers, meaning that *Microraptor* had four wings! This may indicate that living birds evolved from dinosaurs with four wings. Scientists are studying how bird flight evolved, and dinosaurs like *Microraptor* and *Hesperonychus* are critical to this type of research.

Ashley Heers is a graduate student who studies how birds evolved the ability to fly. She uses computer models to study ancient dinosaurs like *Microraptor*. But most importantly, she carefully studies living birds (both in nature and the lab) to better understand their full range of flight speeds and behaviours.

ALEXORNIS

Birds evolved from dinosaurs long before the dinosaurs became extinct. The oldest known bird fossil is still the iconic *Archaeopteryx*, which is about 150 million years old, from Late Jurassic Germany. *Archaeopteryx* is quite advanced. Although it may not have been able to fly as powerfully as living birds, it has a full set of feathers on its wings. This means that birds must have evolved long before *Archaeopteryx*. It is likely that the first birds arose sometime in the Early to Middle Jurassic, maybe as long as 180–200 million years ago.

There are about 10,000 species of living birds. There were many fewer types of birds during the Age of Dinosaurs, but birds were not necessarily rare during this time. New species are being found every year, especially in China, where thousands of bird fossils are preserved in the same rock layers as the famous 'feathered dinosaurs'. All of these discoveries tell us that Mesozoic birds were common and diverse. Some were unusual compared to living species, because they still had teeth in their jaws and long, straight tails that might have been used to steer during flight. Some species even have wings on their legs, just like the dromaeosaurid *Microraptor*.

Luis Chiappe is an Argentine palaeontologist who heads the Dinosaur Institute at the Natural History Museum of Los Angeles, California. Luis is one of the world's experts on birds that lived during the time of dinosaurs. He consulted on *Walking with Dinosaurs: The 3D Movie* by providing information on the anatomy and behaviour of *Alexornis* and the feathered theropods.

During the Mesozoic, one unusual group of birds dominated the skies. These were the enantiornithines, the so-called opposite birds. They were given this name because many features of their skeleton are different from living birds. For example, many species still had teeth and claws on the wings, which living birds lack. Enantiornithines were very common during the time of dinosaurs. Over fifty species have been found. One of these is *Alexornis*.

Unfortunately, very little is actually known about *Alexornis*. Although it stars in *Walking with Dinosaurs: The 3D Movie*, scientists still don't know much about what it ate or how well it could fly. This is because it is only known from a few fossil bones, discovered in the Late Cretaceous rocks of Baja California, Mexico, in the 1970s. But these bones do tell us that *Alexornis* was small, probably about the size of a living finch. Did it behave like a finch? What colour was it? Did it live in places other than Mexico? All of these questions can only be answered with new fossil discoveries.

Jingmai O'Connor is an American scientist who studies the enantiornithines, the group of 'opposite birds' such as *Alexornis* that were common during the Mesozoic.

EDMONTOSAURUS

Edmontosaurus was something like a dinosaur version of a horse. Large herds of these animals roamed across western North America at the end of the Cretaceous, chomping plants and dodging predators like *T. rex*.

At this time, the long-necked sauropod dinosaurs were rare in North America. It was duck-billed hadrosaurids like *Edmontosaurus* that were the largest plant eaters. These animals are distinguished from all other dinosaurs by their unusual skulls, which are very long, packed full of teeth and fronted with a wide beak like that of a duck. *Edmontosaurus* lived in North America in the Cretaceous, and it was among the biggest of the hadrosaurid group. An average adult was about 30 feet long, but some individuals grew to about 40 feet in length, the same size as *T. rex*! Most adults were about 6–10 feet tall at the hips and weighed 3–4 tons.

Hadrosaurids probably became so successful because of their unusual feeding style, which allowed them to grab, chew, and swallow plants very quickly. The hadrosaurid skull is a marvel of evolution.

Albert Prieto-Márquez grew up in Spain and moved to the United States to study dinosaurs. He is a specialist on the anatomy and evolution of the duck-billed hadrosaurids.

The ducklike beak was used to grab plants. Behind the beak was a long region without any teeth. This would have given the tongue space to collect the plant material and send it further back into the mouth, where it could be cut into small pieces by the teeth. Some of the skull bones of hadrosaurids attached only loosely to each other, allowing the lower jaw to move from side to side as well as up and down. Chewing enabled hadrosaurids like *Edmontosaurus* to eat large amounts of food quickly.

The most amazing feature of the skull of *Edmontosaurus* was its teeth. There are about 200 individual teeth inside the jaws. These are packed tightly together into 'dental batteries'. The teeth were so tightly packed that it's almost impossible to recognize each individual tooth. They would have formed a single, long cutting surface to chop plants like a pair of scissors. Dinosaurs could grow new teeth throughout their life, unlike mammals, which only have two sets of teeth. In *Edmontosaurus* the teeth continuously replaced themselves. Scientists call this a 'conveyor-belt' process. Fast replacement was important, because *Edmontosaurus* ate so much and so quickly that its teeth would have been easily worn down.

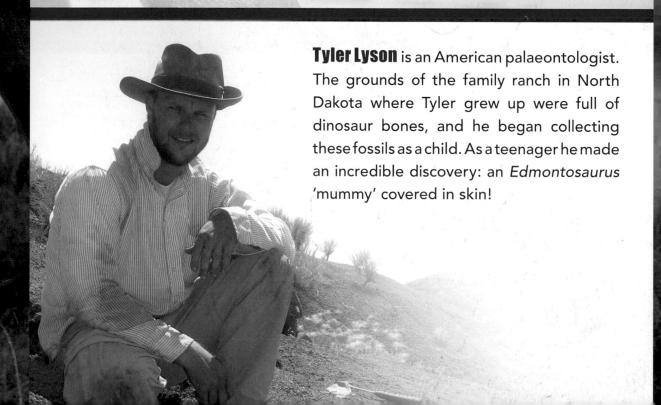

Tyler Lyson is an American palaeontologist. The grounds of the family ranch in North Dakota where Tyler grew up were full of dinosaur bones, and he began collecting these fossils as a child. As a teenager he made an incredible discovery: an *Edmontosaurus* 'mummy' covered in skin!

Hadrosaurids like *Edmontosaurus* could also move very fast, at least compared to most other dinosaurs. *Edmontosaurus* had long, muscular legs. Some computer models predict that it could have run at about the same speed as *T. rex*, and perhaps even faster. It probably wasn't unusual for a hadrosaurid to race across the plains at speeds of 20–25 miles per hour. When moving at such speeds, *Edmontosaurus* probably ran using only its two hind limbs. But when walking more slowly, it probably stood on all fours. The hands of *Edmontosaurus* have small hooves on the end of the fingers, as do the feet. Hooves are seen in many modern-day running animals like horses and sheep.

Edmontosaurus could probably run fast for a reason. These duck-billed dinosaurs lived in the same ecosystems as *T. rex*. Scientists know that *T. rex* had a taste for *Edmontosaurus*, because *Edmontosaurus* bones have been found covered in bite marks that match the size and shape of *T. rex* teeth. Because *Edmontosaurus* did not have any spikes, clubs or other defensive weapons, it probably relied mostly on its speed to protect itself from a *T. rex* attack.

Hadrosaurids like *Edmontosaurus* were probably very good parents. A close relative of *Edmontosaurus* is *Maiasaura*, whose name means 'good mother lizard'. Scientists have discovered huge prehistoric nesting

Natalia Rybczynski is a Canadian palaeontologist who studies biomechanics: the science of how organisms move and function. She led a team that built a three-dimensional computer model of a hadrosaurid skull. They used this model to study how hadrosaurids fed.

grounds where *Maiasaura* mothers (and maybe fathers) would gather together to lay eggs and raise their hatchlings.

Fossils of *Edmontosaurus* are very common. They are found in latest Cretaceous rocks across western North America, especially in Alberta, Canada and the American states of Montana and South Dakota.

Amazingly, even a few *Edmontosaurus* mummies have been found! These remarkable fossils were preserved in a weird way. Somehow, the whole body of the animal dried out before it was buried, which meant that the skin, muscles and even some internal organs could be preserved. These mummies tell scientists that the skin of *Edmontosaurus* was covered in small scales and the beak was made of keratin, the same substance as in our fingernails. Some mummies even preserve the animal's last meal as bits of shredded leaves and twigs found inside the gut.

Nicolás Campione is a young Canadian palaeontologist who studies duck-billed dinosaurs. He is particularly interested in predicting the weight of hadrosaurids and other dinosaurs based on the size and shape of their bones.

PARKSOSAURUS

Parksosaurus did not look very impressive. It was small, much smaller than a human. It didn't have any big spikes or plates on its skeleton, or any decorative crests on its skull. It's easy to forget about dinosaurs like *Parksosaurus*. But in fact, there were many small dinosaurs of this kind. They were important components of dinosaur ecosystems. And scientists are rapidly learning more about them as more fossils are being found.

The problem with dinosaurs like *Parksosaurus* is that their fossils are rare, so palaeontologists don't have much material to study. The rarity of fossils is almost certainly due to one reason: the skeletons of *Parksosaurus* and similar dinosaurs were small and fragile. Their bones easily broke apart after death. It is difficult for these types of skeletons to be preserved as fossils.

Although its fossils are rare, *Parksosaurus* was probably a common animal back in Late Cretaceous North America. It lived in what is present-day Canada, about 73–70 million years ago. *Parksosaurus* was about the size of a very large dog: about 6 feet long, 30 inches high at the hips, and weighing about 90–110 pounds.

Richard Butler is a British palaeontologist who studies dinosaurs at the University of Birmingham. His research focuses on the anatomy and family tree of small plant-eating dinosaurs like *Parksosaurus*.

Sarah Werning recently finished her graduate studies at the University of California, Berkeley. Sarah studies dinosaur growth by looking at bones under the microscope. She counts growth lines to determine how old a dinosaur was when it died.

Parksosaurus, *Thescelosaurus* and their close relatives are classified together in the dinosaur group Hypsilophodontidae. Scientists still know very little about these dinosaurs, but the known fossils make it clear that they ate plants and could run fast. Their skulls are filled with many small, leaf-shaped teeth. The leaflike shape of the teeth is due to the presence of large 'denticles' along the edges of the teeth. These were used to grind and cut plant material. Hypsilophodontids were distant relatives of the duck-billed hadrosaurids like *Edmontosaurus*. But they didn't have the powerful dental batteries of hadrosaurids, in which many teeth are packed together to create a scissor-like cutting surface. Instead, *Parksosaurus* had fewer and more simple teeth, and probably was restricted to eating low-growing plants like ferns and small shrubs.

The first fossils of *Parksosaurus* were found in the 1920s in Alberta, along the picturesque Red Deer River.

ANKYLOSAURUS

Ankylosaurus looked something like a military tank. That is the simplest analogy to describe this most bizarre type of dinosaur. Its entire body was covered with thick, bony armour. The end of its tail was a giant club that could be swung from side to side. This was a dinosaur you wouldn't want to mess with. It lived alongside *Tyrannosaurus rex*, but even the fearsome tyrant dinosaur king probably avoided *Ankylosaurus* at all costs. At the very least, a *Tyrannosaurus rex* may have broken its teeth trying to slice through the tough armour. And if it was really unlucky, it may have been knocked over – or even worse, killed – by a blow from the tail club.

Ankylosaurus was a large and strong animal. Adults were probably about 19–26 feet long, about 6 feet tall at the hip, and weighed 5–6 tons. They walked on all fours and probably moved very slowly, at most just a few miles per hour. A sturdy, armoured animal like *Ankylosaurus* didn't need to run fast to escape from predators. If it was threatened it could probably just hunker down and wait for a predator to exhaust itself trying to break through the bony armour. Some living armoured animals like armadillos behave this way.

The armour of *Ankylosaurus* was incredible. Its protective coat was formed by several individual pieces of bone called osteoderms, which were buried inside the skin. All of these osteoderms fit together

Victoria Arbour is a Canadian palaeontology student. She is an expert on armoured dinosaurs like *Ankylosaurus*. Victoria studies the skeletons of these weird dinosaurs to better understand how they moved and grew. Victoria consulted on *Walking with Dinosaurs: The 3D Movie* by giving the animators advice on the anatomy and behaviour of *Ankylosaurus*.

to create an armour sheath that covered the neck, back and hips of *Ankylosaurus*. Smaller osteoderms were probably also present on the arms, legs and tail. Even the skull was protected by an interlocking array of osteoderms.

The club at the end of the tail was also made of osteoderms, which fused together with the bones of the tail to create a huge, heavy mass. The club was about the same size as the skull. It was heavy like a bowling ball. Computer models have shown that animals like *Ankylosaurus* could swing their clubs at fast speeds, quick and powerful enough to break the bones of any predator or rival they came into contact with.

Ankylosaurus is a member of a larger group of dinosaurs called the ankylosaurs. This group was named for *Ankylosaurus* itself, which was one of the first armoured dinosaurs discovered. All ankylosaurs walked slowly on four legs, had some type of bony armour and ate plants. Their skulls were short and wide, and their jaws were filled with tiny teeth. They probably couldn't chew their food and must have specialized in small plants that lived near the ground.

Ankylosaurus lived in North America at the very end of the Cretaceous Period. It wasn't a particularly common dinosaur, at least compared to the ceratopsids and hadrosaurids. While the ceratopsids and hadrosaurids formed huge herds with hundreds or thousands of individuals travelling together, ankylosaurs may have been more solitary animals. There are no bone beds that preserve the skeletons of hundreds of ankylosaurs in Late Cretaceous North America. But there are such bone beds from other parts of the world, suggesting that at least some ankylosaurs may have been social animals that formed herds.

Paul Barrett is the lead dinosaur palaeontologist at London's famous Natural History Museum. He studies plant-eating dinosaurs like *Ankylosaurus* and its close relatives. He described a new species of ankylosaur from China and has studied how these dinosaurs fed and what types of plants they ate.

AZHDARCHID PTEROSAURS

During the last few million years of the Cretaceous, when *Tyrannosaurus* stalked herds of duck-billed dinosaurs across the plains and river valleys of North America, an amazing group of flying reptiles dominated the skies.

Pterosaurs first appeared in the Late Triassic – along with their close relatives the dinosaurs. By the end of the Cretaceous, one group of pterosaurs, the Azhdarchidae, had given rise to creatures of spectacular size.

Azhdarchid pterosaurs such as *Quetzalcoatlus* and *Hatzegopteryx* were true prehistoric dragons – flying reptiles that, with wingspans of 32–42 feet, were larger than a small plane! One of the smaller azhdarchids, *Montanazhdarcho*, 'only' had a wingspan of about 8 feet. In comparison, the largest wingspan of any living bird is about 11 feet.

Although *Quetzalcoatlus* and *Hatzegopteryx* were enormous, they probably didn't weigh very much. Scientists think that the entire body weighed about 440–550 pounds, a fraction of what a *Tyrannosaurus* or *Edmontosaurus* would weigh.

How could such huge animals be so light? Like all pterosaurs, their bones were mostly hollow inside. This makes sense. If the bones were heavy and solid, then the body of giant azhdarchids would have been too bulky and massive to fly.

In fact, some scientists think that even a 440–550 pound *Hatzegopteryx* might have been too heavy to fly. One idea is that it could have evolved from flying ancestors but lost the ability to take to the air, much like the modern-day ostrich. This is a controversial idea and is still being debated by scientists. If *Hatzegopteryx* could not fly, it might have been a fierce predator that hunted on the ground.

Azhdarchid pterosaurs had a long skull with a sharp, pointed beak. The skull was probably topped by a thin crest, which was used to attract mates. The neck was long and the forearms were modified into wings – although they were completely different to those of a bird. While a bird wing is mostly made up of feathers which attach to the bones of the arm, a pterosaur wing is a sheet of skin supported from a single enlarged finger – equivalent to our ring finger.

The first fossils of *Quetzalcoatlus* were discovered in Texas in the early 1970s in rocks formed right at the end of the Cretaceous, about 68 million years ago. *Hatzegopteryx* fossils were found more recently, in Romania. It also lived during the very latest Cretaceous. So it seems that enormous flying pterosaurs were actually quite common all over the world during the last few million years of the dinosaurs.

Michael Habib is an American palaeontologist and biologist who studies how pterosaurs fly. He uses computer models and mathematical equations to estimate the speed of flying animals.

Many movies and books mistakenly call pterosaurs dinosaurs, but this is not true. They are not dinosaurs because they do not possess the defining features of dinosaurs, such as an open hip socket and large muscles on the upper arm bone. Instead, pterosaurs were one of many peculiar reptile groups that were very successful during the Mesozoic but are extinct today.

Mark Witton is a British palaeontologist who is fascinated with pterosaurs. He is also an artist who is widely respected for his beautiful, vivid drawings of dinosaurs and other prehistoric creatures. Mark worked on *Walking with Dinosaurs: The 3D Movie* by creating the original drawings used to make the azhdarchid pterosaur CGI model and providing fact files on all of the characters that were used by the animators to ensure that the anatomy and behaviour of the movie dinosaurs were scientifically accurate.

ALPHADON

The Mesozoic Era was the Age of Dinosaurs. Dinosaurs were the dominant creatures on land and lived across the globe. Other groups like crocodiles, lizards and mammals lived alongside the dinosaurs. But it is often said that these groups were overshadowed by the dinosaurs, restricted to only a few species that were small and not very common. We often hear this story about mammals in particular.

As with many stories about fossils, this story about mammal evolution is partially true and partially false. It is true that mammals and dinosaurs originated at the same time, during that exciting period after the end-Permian extinction in which new types of animals were quickly evolving and spreading around the world. So that means it's true that mammals lived alongside dinosaurs during the entire time that dinosaurs dominated the planet. It is also true that mammals weren't very big during this time, and they certainly didn't have the great range of diets and lifestyles that they have today.

But mammals were not necessarily rare during the time of dinosaurs. There were many species, and they lived across the planet. Most of these mammals were quite small, but some got to be as large as dogs.

One group of mammals that were very common during the

Thomas Williamson is a palaeontologist who works in New Mexico. He is an expert on fossil mammals. He has studied Cretaceous marsupials like *Alphadon* and built a family tree for the group.

Mesozoic Era were the marsupials. Marsupials are still alive today. Some examples are koalas and kangaroos. They give birth to tiny babies that then continue to grow inside a pouch on the mother.

Alphadon was a type of marsupial that lived in North America during the latest Cretaceous period, about 70–66 million years ago. It is known almost entirely from fossilized teeth, which are just a few millimetres long. Scientists can only guess at the appearance of the rest of the skeleton, but based on the size of its teeth it was likely that *Alphadon* was about as big as a rat. Its teeth are similar to those of modern-day

Anne Weil is an American palaeontologist. Anne studies a strange group of mammals called the multituberculates. These mammals were very common during the Age of Dinosaurs but are extinct today. They looked like, and probably behaved like, living rats and mice.

omnivorous mammals, which eat both plants and meat. Marsupials like *Alphadon* were very common during the Late Cretaceous Period, but were devastated by the end-Cretaceous extinction that killed off the dinosaurs. *Alphadon* itself went extinct, as did most of its close relatives. Only a few marsupials survived, which evolved into the kangaroos and possums of today's world.

DINOSAUR EXTINCTION

Dinosaurs were amazing animals. They dominated the planet like nothing that had ever lived before them. Dinosaurs thrived for over 150 million years. They evolved into thousands of species, which lived in nearly every type of environment and all across the globe.

Why did all of the dinosaurs, except for birds, become extinct? This is one of the oldest and most controversial questions in palaeontology. The first scientists to discover dinosaurs made the obvious observation that these giant reptile-like creatures were no longer alive today. But did they die out quickly, as the result of a global catastrophe? Or did they slowly fade away into extinction? What caused their extinction?

There are a few things about the dinosaur extinction that we do know. Scientists are sure that dinosaurs became extinct about 66 million years ago. Dinosaur fossils disappear at this time, all across the world. Rocks that were formed after 66 million years ago never contain dinosaur fossils. Something else also happened 66 million years ago. A huge asteroid about 6 miles wide smashed into present-day Mexico. There is a big crater, nearly 124 miles wide, that formed when the asteroid hit.

This asteroid collision was devastating. It didn't only affect those dinosaurs and other species living in Mexico – it caused destruction across the entire planet. The impact caused vast amounts of dirt and dust to be launched into the atmosphere. This would have created a thick, black cloud that blocked out the sun for days, months or maybe even years. This created a deadly domino effect. Without sunlight

Graeme Lloyd is a British scientist who studies the evolution of dinosaurs. He compiles large databases of information on how dinosaurs changed over time – how many species there were at certain times, which groups these species belonged to, and how large these dinosaurs were.

most plants could not grow. Without plants to eat, herbivorous animals would begin to die. And without plant eaters, meat-eating dinosaurs would also starve to death. The remnants of this huge dust cloud are found today as a thin layer of clay that is 66 million years old. It is found all around the world, and dinosaur bones are not found above it.

The asteroid would have caused other problems as well. Because it hit near the ocean, the asteroid triggered monster tidal waves that might have been several storeys high. These swept across the world's oceans, destroying all land and life in their path. The asteroid also caused earthquakes, probably more powerful than any human has ever experienced. Wildfires spread across the land, burning down forests and poisoning the atmosphere with smoke. All of these things would have decimated the dinosaurs and other animals and plants living across the world.

It is important to note that this extinction story is not supported by every scientist. An asteroid hit the Earth 66 million years ago. That is a fact. But some scientists don't think this asteroid was big enough to cause all of the environmental destruction described above, or to kill off an entire group like the dinosaurs. There were also some other weird things happening at the end of the Cretaceous Period, around the same time dinosaurs became extinct. Huge volcanic eruptions were occurring in present-day India. These were not the quick, explosive

Jonathan Mitchell is a graduate student in Chicago who studies how dinosaurs fit into their larger ecosystems. He has compiled information on Late Cretaceous dinosaurs and other species living alongside them.

volcanic eruptions that we are used to in today's world. Instead, these eruptions produced a slow, steady flow of lava for thousands, or maybe even millions, of years. Today the remains of this lava covers over 190,000 square miles in India! This much lava would have produced a lot of toxic gas, which could have polluted the atmosphere and poisoned the dinosaurs.

Scientists continue to debate whether an asteroid or volcanoes were responsible for the death of the dinosaurs. Or maybe the volcanoes and asteroid worked together in tandem. Maybe the volcanic eruptions weakened dinosaurs by making it harder to grow and reproduce, and then the asteroid delivered the final killing blow. Or maybe something else entirely caused the extinction? Ultimately, we may never know for sure.

No matter how the dinosaurs became extinct, the fact is that they are gone. Birds, their descendants, survived and remain diverse and successful today. Mammals made it through the extinction as well. Not many species, but enough to keep the mammals going through such a destructive time. Within a few thousand years mammals began to evolve at incredible speed. Entirely new groups of mammals came on to the scene. In essence, mammals became the new dinosaurs. They became the dominant creatures on land. Humans are part of this evolutionary explosion of mammals. Without the extinction of the dinosaurs, we probably wouldn't be here.

Steve Brusatte is a palaeontologist and research fellow at the University of Edinburgh in the United Kingdom. He studies the anatomy, genealogy and evolution of dinosaurs and other fossil animals with backbones. Steve's particular research interests are the origin of dinosaurs and the evolution of birds from carnivorous dinosaurs. He has a PhD from Columbia University and degrees from the University of Chicago and University of Bristol. He has written over sixty scientific papers, published four books (including the coffee table book *Dinosaurs* and the technical volume *Dinosaur Palaeobiology*), and has described over ten new species of fossil animals. He has done fieldwork in Britain, China, Lithuania, Poland, Portugal, Romania and the United States. His research is profiled often in the popular press and he is a 'resident palaeontologist' on the *Walking with Dinosaurs: The 3D Movie* team.

INTRODUCTION

ALL-CONQUERING Rangers proved, yet again in season 1992/93, that they were undoubtedly in a league of their own . . . Simply The Best!

A 5th successive Championship (the club's first 'Five-in-a-Row' in over sixty years) and the coveted 'Treble' of League Cup, League Championship and Scottish Cup for the first time since 1978, underlined the Ibrox domestic supremacy. The 26th Scottish Cup victory brought the season to a glorious ending.

European glory had also beckoned as Rangers, after a stunning run, came so close to gracing the Final of the prestigious European Cup.

Yes, it was, indeed, a 'Wonder Year', full of glorious occasions – reason enough for reliving them once again in this year's Annual.

Written by Douglas G. Russell
and
Edited by John Traynor
Compiling Editors of 'Blue Heaven'
Editors of Rangers Annuals Nos. 1, 2 & 3

CONTENTS

THE BEST

'The Battle

SUPPORTERS streaming out of Ibrox after the first leg European tie against Leeds were understandably hopeful for the return match. After all, Rangers had still won 2-1 on the night despite losing a goal in the first minute.

Needless to say, the English media had by this time written off Rangers' chances of progressing further in the tournament — Leeds would destroy them at home.

Little did anyone realise, however, what high drama would unfold at Elland Road. We would be privileged to witness a glorious chapter in Rangers history being written on English soil as the Ibrox club took their place alongside the elite of Europe in the latter stages of the European Cup.

The pre-match plans of Leeds manager, Howard Wilkinson, lay in tatters after only three minutes when Mark Hateley's vicious strike stunned the capacity crowd into complete silence. Except, of course, for the 'few' Rangers fans in the crowd.

Some of the English observers had the audacity to call Mark's goal a fluke. Suffice to say, that this so-called 'fluke' must rank as a major contender for THE goal of this and many other seasons!

Rangers were now 3-1 ahead on aggregate and began to play like a team convinced of their right to progress in the tournament.

The game was emphatically ended as a contest early in the second half following a beautifully-orchestrated move down the left involving Durrant and Hateley — the big man's curling cross being superbly headed home by 'Super' himself. It was all over, even allowing for Cantona's consolation goal with five minutes remaining.

OF TIMES

of Britain'

The 'Blues Brothers' European Tour in the Champions' League was soon to hit the road. Many great nights would 'Follow, Follow' but nothing could compare to this — the memories of which will last a lifetime. Thank you, Rangers. ■

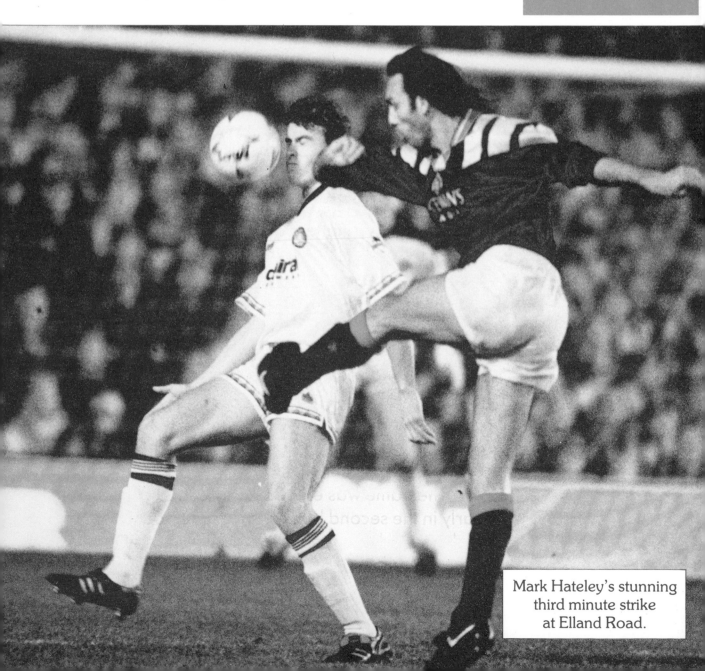

Mark Hateley's stunning third minute strike at Elland Road.

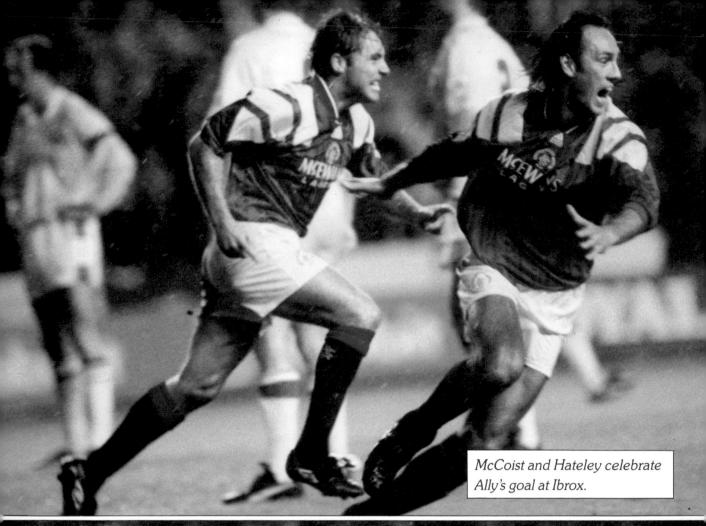

McCoist and Hateley celebrate Ally's goal at Ibrox.

It's all over!

THE RIGHT

Scottish Cup Final, Saturday 29th May 1993

ABERDEEN 1
Richardson (78mins)

RANGERS 2
Murray (22 mins)
Hateley (42 mins)

THE SCRIPTWRITERS had got it right – the 1993 Cup Final would be contested by Scotland's top two teams of Rangers and Aberdeen. The 'Dons' had earlier tracked the 'Light Blues' Championship trail all season but to no avail.

It was appropriate, therefore, that the team from the North should now stand between Rangers and the Ibrox quest for that elusive 'Treble' of domestic honours.

A surprising number of neutrals had written off Rangers after such an ardous season and the recent emotional exit from Europe, installing Aberdeen as pre-match favourites. Certainly the 'Reds' started the game exceptionally well, with a Brian Grant shot shaving Goram's post in only the second minute.

Gradually, though, as had happened so many times throughout the season, Rangers effortlessly stepped up a gear and almost inevitably scored to rip the heart out of the opposition.

An inviting Stuart McCall cross into the box was completely missed by Aberdeen's Brian Irvine and fell to the youngest man on the park, Neil Murray. Trying desperately to recover and make amends for his initial error, Irvine only succeeded in diverting Murray's cross-shot to the far post past the helpless Snelders in goal. Painful memories of the Skol Cup Final must have come flooding back to the Aberdeen players and fans!

STUFF

There was no such dubiety concerning Rangers' second goal as the first half drew to a close. The move was started and finished by the majestic Mark Hateley: a pulverising burst of speed, a deftly-measured through ball from Ian Durrant and an absolute peach of a strike from a tight angle, when Aberdeen were probably anticipating the cut-back. Certainly, this beautifully-executed goal was fit to win any competition and it assuredly destined the Cup once more for the Ibrox Trophy Room.

Aberdeen's Richardson (via a wicked John Brown deflection) pulled one back with 12 minutes to go but, as with Airdrie last year, it was a case of too little, too late.

The Rangers players had once again risen to the occasion and no-one could begrudge them their victory. Call it 'True Grit', 'Hearts of Fire' or 'The Right Stuff', they certainly possessed something out of the ordinary.

Players and fans alike celebrated long into the Glasgow night. It had been another perfect day. ∎

RANGERS: Goram,   McCall,
D. Robertson,   Gough,   McPherson
Brown,   Murray,   Ferguson
Durrant,   Hateley,   Huistra
(Pressley 88 mins)

Neil Murray strikes the first goal.

Hateley's stunning decider.

BOMBER

JOHN BROWN

IT WILL be a long time before the emotional aftermath of Rangers' final 'Champions League' game at Ibrox against CSKA Moscow is forgotten. It was fitting that John Brown would throw his jersey to fans in the enclosure . . . . after all, he has been a 'Gers supporter all his days.

'Bomber' had a superb '92/'93 season with a host of solid, reliable and committed defensive displays. Indeed, in the eyes of many, he was nothing short of heroic for Rangers throughout the club's extended European campaign.

When his playing days are eventually at an end, it would be no great surprise to find John back amongst the 'Bears' following his beloved team. ■

1992/93 Stats-at-a-Glance

Competition	Appearances	Goals
Premier League	39	4
Skol Cup	3 (2)	-
Scottish Cup	5	-
Europe	10	-
Total	57	4

Figures in brackets denote subsititute appearances

Celtic are Put to the Sword

Premier League, 7th November 1992
CELTIC 0   **RANGERS 1**
Durrant (33 mins)

FEW TEAMS would relish facing Celtic at Parkhead only three days after a major European tie away from home against the current English Champions. This was the prospect that faced Rangers, however, after their historic victory at Elland Road in the European Cup.

That Celtic enjoyed the bulk of the play, with greater possession and chances, could not be denied but Ian Durrant's first half goal ensured that the Ibrox club would move six points clear of their oldest rivals in the Championship race. The cause had not been helped by the loss of both central defenders, John Brown and Richard Gough, during the game itself but these difficulties only seemed to strengthen Rangers' resolve.

Andy Goram was once again immense, the master of all he surveyed.

RANGERS: Goram, McCall, D. Robertson
Gough (Mikhailitchenko 69 mins), McPherson
Brown (Huistra 45 mins), Gordon, Ferguson
McCoist, Hateley, Durrant

Ally waits to congratulate Ian Durrant.

THE CUTTING EDGE

Premier League, 2nd January 1993

RANGERS 1   **CELTIC** 0
Steven (33 mins)

AS WITH the previous encounter, neutrals observed that Celtic enjoyed the bulk of play. Few would argue that point or, more significantly, that Rangers did what really mattered – put the ball in the net!

On this occasion, Trevor Steven's purposeful header was enough to secure the points. Yet again, Andy Goram was in inspirational form. It was becoming a habit. ■

> RANGERS: Goram, McCall, D. Robertson Gough, McPherson, Brown, Steven, Ferguson, Gordon, Hateley, Durrant   (Mikhailitchenko 72 mins)

Ian Durrant, scorer of the winning goal at Parkhead in November, seen here celebrating his stunning equaliser at Ibrox in the first 'Old Firm' match of last season. His delight is obvious!

HIT·MAN

RARELY does a player provide more than enough memories in one season to last a lifetime. Quite simply, Mark Hateley was one such man in season 1992/93.

Remember . . . . the magnificent left foot volley from 25 yards at Elland Road against Leeds in the European Cup, the ball nestling securely in the back of the net even before 'keeper Lukic had returned to Earth . . . . the inch perfect curling cross for Ally's diving header and goal No.2 in the same game . . . . Mark's own headed equaliser against Marseille with some eight minutes left to play that almost took the roof off Ibrox . . . . another perfect header against Aberdeen at Pittodrie in February to secure the points and severely dent the Dons' title challenge . . . . the burst of pace, superb run and sweet low shot from an acute angle for Rangers' second and decisive Cup Final goal.

Looking back, the list of highlights seems almost endless. It was, indeed a privilege to have watched a supreme striker at the peak of his ability. ∎

HATELEY

Ian Ferguson v Dundee

There

is

Nothing

David Robertson v St. Johnstone

like a

David Hagen v Hibs

Goal!

Ally McCoist v Motherwell

Born to Run

SOME players develop an affinity with a club's supporters almost immediately. Others never quite seem to break down that invisible barrier. Stuart McCall certainly joined the former category very soon after signing for Rangers, the Ibrox legions realising from the outset that here, indeed, was a man who would play for the jersey till he dropped.

Amongst many inspirational performances last term were McCall's displays in the Skol Cup Final victory over Aberdeen (when he also scored the first goal) and the 1-0 Parkhead victory against Celtic in which he filled the right back position.

The record-breaking Rangers squad of season 1992/93 was imbued throughout with tremendous spirit. As much as anyone, this never-say-die attitude was typified by Stuart McCall. ■

1992/93 Stats-at-a-Glance

Competition	Appearances	Goals
Premier League	34 (1)	5
Skol Cup	4	1
Scottish Cup	5	-
Europe	9	-
Total	53 (1)	6

Figures in brackets denote subsitute appearances

Blues Brothers

McCall and McPherson celebrate at Elland Road.

EUROPEAN TOUR

Ian Durrant's opener at Ibrox against Bruges.

MAYBE it was Ally's tears. Certainly, something touched an emotion deep inside, the night Rangers' brave European campaign came to an end.

The Ibrox legions had remained to a man to applaud their heroes from the field, remembering with pride Elland Road, the Velodrome and a host of marvellous, memorable moments.

It was, indeed, the best of times. ■

27

Blues Brothers EUROPEAN TOUR

Below: Rangers v Bruges. Scott Nisbet enjoys his 'wonder' goal at Ibrox

Opposite: Above, Rangers v Leeds. Goal No. 2 courtesy of 'Super' himself.
Below, Rangers v Marseille. Ian Durrant bursts through the French rearguard.

The goal that almost took the roof off Ibrox.
Mark Hateley's late equaliser against Marseille.

Rangers v CSKA Moscow. One of the many agonisingly close things.

The end of a Dream.

SUPER!

PROBABLY one of the most surprising aspects of Rangers' unbeaten European run was that Ally McCoist never actually scored in the 'Champions League' run of matches against the elite of Europe. His contribution and work rate were, none the less, immense in creating room for others to score.

As it was, throughout the year, Ally's front-line partnership with Mark Hateley yielded an amazing 78 goals of which 'Attila' netted just 29.

'Coisty's' sensational strike rate of 49 goals in all competitions comprised 34 in the Premier League, 8 in the Skol Cup, 5 in the Scottish Cup and those two most memorable goals against Leeds home and away in the 2nd round of the European Cup.

No doubt this Super Tally would have been even greater had it not been for the tragic leg break when playing for Scotland which prematurely ended McCoist's 1992/93 season.

Regardless of that, however, his 34 League goals still enabled him to claim Europe's 'Golden Boot' award (by a single goal from A.E.K. striker Vasillis Dimitridias) for the second year running.

Few players seem to take greater pleasure in scoring. There can be no more heartwarming experience on a typical Scottish winter's day (you know... on the cool side, with a slight drizzle in the air) than to see Ally score and literally explode with unbridled joy.

As they say in the song, "Still crazy after all these years". ∎

Super....

Super!

Hearts of Fire

Skol Cup Final, 25th October 1992

RANGERS 2   ABERDEEN 1

McCall (14 mins)
Smith (o.g. 114 mins)

JUST MAYBE the odds were against Rangers. This first final of the season was to be played only four days after the hard-earned and exhausting victory over Leeds United in the Glasgow leg of their European Cup tie.

Many neutrals questioned whether the 'Light Blues' could lift themselves so soon for such an important game. But as was to be proved on many memorable occasions in the coming months, this was a truly exceptional Rangers team. In fact, by the following summer, one that would rightfully have earned a place alongside the great sides of days gone by.

Stuart McCall's early first half goal (after a pass-back mistake) had been cancelled out by Duncan Shearer's 62nd minute equaliser, albeit against the run of play.

Although it was eventually decided in extra time by an own goal from defender Gary Smith, the game itself seemed to epitomise Rangers' will to win. There was no doubt that they finished by far the stronger team even though both the influential Richard Gough and Trevor Steven had been lost earlier through injury.

The Skol and League Cups were returning to the Ibrox Trophy Room. A great start and only the beginning – THE BEST WAS YET TO COME. ■

RANGERS: Goram, McCall, D. Robertson Gough, (Mikhailitchenko 65 mins), McPherson, Brown, Steven (Gordon 58 mins), Ferguson, McCoist, Hateley, Durrant.

Broken Hearts

Scottish Cup Semi-Final, Saturday 3rd April 1993

RANGERS 2   HEARTS 1
McPherson (70mins)
McCoist (75 mins)

CUP SEMI-FINALS can be notoriously dour affairs; understandably with so much at stake for both clubs. Glory beckons for the winner, whereas the losers are easily forgotten.

Rangers were not only playing for a place in the Final but also a possible domestic 'Treble'. However, with twenty minutes remaining and Hearts a goal up, they looked out of it. But as was shown on so many previous occasions from Bruges and beyond, this Rangers team would not lie down.

Following a Trevor Steven corner, Dave McPherson hammered home the equaliser, to his obvious delight in scoring against his former club. The winner, courtesy of 'Super', followed five minutes later when Ally displayed his priceless speed of thought and action with a typical touch of opportunism to knock the ball over the advancing Hearts 'keeper, Nicky Walker.

Rangers were through to the Final for the second year in succession and would return to Parkhead for that May date. They were now on the verge of something very special – only 4 teams before in the Club's proud history had completed the domestic 'Treble'.

To be No. 5 in the year of 'Five-in-a-Row' certainly had a ring to it. ∎

'Fergie' in typical midfield action

Dave McPherson's equaliser

PHOTO FUN QUIZ

Answers on Page 64

1. Who is the possessor of this very fine pair of legs?

★ ★ ★

2. Check the natty suede jacket and the speedboat! Who is it?

★ ★ ★

3. Ally's 'medical attendants' are Justin Fashanu and which World Champion who is, like Rangers, 'Simply the Best'?

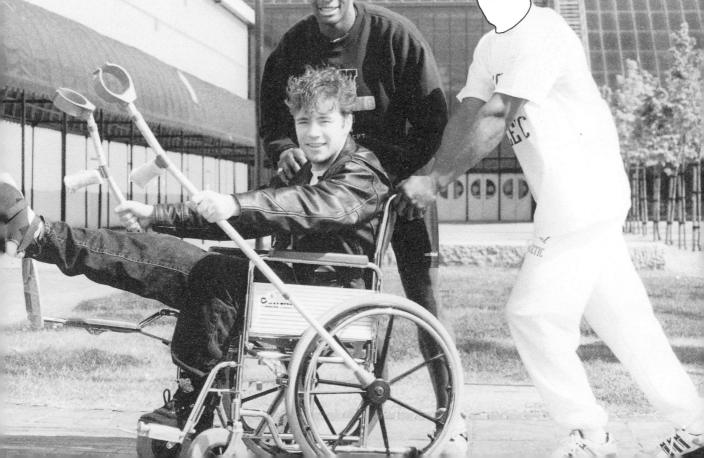

THE 1 AND ONLY

IN a season full of accolades, Andy Goram was awarded both the Scottish Sportswriters' and the Scottish Players Union 'Player of the Year' prizes, two of the most prestigious honours in our game.

Few would disagree with these awards, as the influential goalkeeper was certainly one of the major factors in Rangers' remarkable European campaign (remember how he broke the heart of Leeds at Elland Road?) and quite magnificent record-breaking unbeaten run of 44 games in season 1992/93.

Probably one of the most encouraging aspects is that at age 29, Andy is not yet, in theory, at his peak as a goalkeeper. The mind, as they say, boggles!

It could well be that in years to come, Andy Goram will be spoken about in the same reverential tones as the legendary Jerry Dawson, one of Rangers' finest-ever between the posts. ■

In the final home league game of the season against Dundee United, the Rangers No. 1 kept another clean sheet, one of his 17 Premier league shut-outs from 34 matches. It was unfortunate that Andy had to miss the start of season 1993/94, due to major knee surgery in the U.S.A. during the close season.

Andy celebrates Ian Durrant's goal against Bruges at Ibrox.

They say it's all over......
.... IT IS NOW !

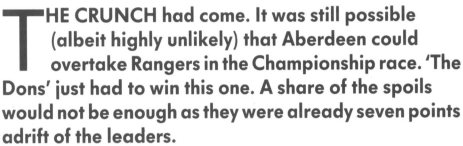

Premier League, 30th March 1993

RANGERS   2   **ABERDEEN   0**
Ferguson (65 mins)
McCoist (89 mins)

THE CRUNCH had come. It was still possible (albeit highly unlikely) that Aberdeen could overtake Rangers in the Championship race. 'The Dons' just had to win this one. A share of the spoils would not be enough as they were already seven points adrift of the leaders.

Full credit to the team from the north, however, for hanging in when all others had faded into obscurity as the Rangers bandwagon continued its relentless pursuit of a record 'Five-in-a-Row' Premier League titles.

Although both teams created chances in the first period, the half ended scoreless. The deadlock was broken in 65 minutes with a quite magnificent 25 yard low drive from Ian Ferguson. Ibrox erupted. Maybe it was appropriate that 'Fergie' scored this important goal, as he had worked tirelessly for the cause all season and was now due the accolades. 'Super' made doubly sure in the dying minutes and it was all over. The fire of Aberdeen's challenge had finally been extinguished.

Rangers were now nine points clear and would eventually secure the Championship by that very margin. Somewhere on the horizon, however, was the small matter of Marseille at the Velodrome Stadium and later still, Aberdeen (again) in the Scottish Cup Final as Rangers chased that elusive 'Treble'

But these would be stories for other days. ■

46

Ally and Mark celebrate Goal No.2

THE SWEETEST

Premier League, 1st May 1993

AIRDRIE 0   **RANGERS 1**
McSwegan (46 mins)

IN BOTH 1991 and 1992, the deed was done at Ibrox. This season there would be a break with tradition – the Premier League Championship would be realised away from home.... at Broomfield. The feeling was just as sweet, none the less.

A huge Rangers travelling support had arrived in Airdrie in party mood. The day was tinged with sadness, however, as Scotland's top goalscorer was missing after suffering that tragic leg-break in Portugal during the World Cup qualifying match.

It was maybe appropriate that 'Super's' replacement on the day, Gary McSwegan (now with Notts County in the English First Division) should score the only goal of the game early in the second half after a delightful ball into the Airdrie penalty area from Mark Hateley.

Not a classic encounter by any means and Airdrie would soon be condemned to relegation and First Division football. But for Rangers it was another milestone, Title No. 43 and that sweet Championship feeling once again.

And in the end, Ally made an 'appearance' after all – as a cardboard cut-out during the players' lap of honour! ∎

RANGERS: Goram, McCall, D. Robertson, Gough, McPherson, Brown, Murray, Ferguson, McSwegan, Hateley, Huistra.

FEELING

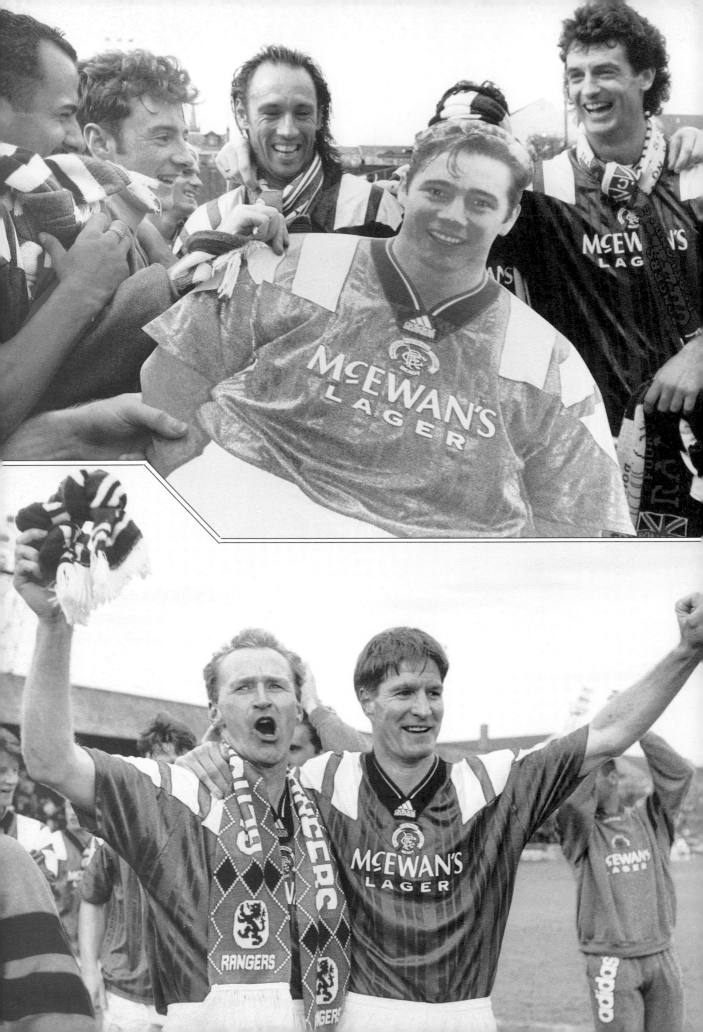

Gary McSwegan's winning goal against Airdrie to clinch the Premier League title

BLUE, WHITE

FEW WILL forget Ian Durrant's stunning equaliser against Marseille in the hostile atmosphere of the Velodrome, thus ensuring that Rangers became the first visitors in 15 European ties to avoid defeat there.

This was the brave midfielder's third goal in the thrilling 1992/93 European Cup campaign, his other strikes being the away goal against Danish Champions, Lyngby, in the September '92 first-round match and Rangers' opening goal against Bruges of Belgium in the Champions' League victory of March '93.

No doubt "Durranty" would also remind us that it was from his corner kick that Leeds' keeper John Lukic punched the ball into his own net to equalise against the English Champions during that memorable 'Battle of Britain' first-leg at Ibrox.

It was one of the season's true (blue) joys to witness Ian back in first team action on a regular basis four years after his horrific knee injury, culminating in the 'Man of the Match' award for a supreme performance in the treble-clinching 1993 Scottish Cup Final victory over Aberdeen. ■

1992/93 Stats-at-a-Glance

Competition	Appearances	Goals
Premier League	19 (11)	3
Skol Cup	5	1
Scottish Cup	3 (2)	-
Europe	9	3
Total	36 (13)	7

Figures in brackets denote subsititute appearances

....DYNAMITE!

Durrant displays some of his skills while in training with the Scotland squad.

HAIL THE

Premier League, 8th May 1993

RANGERS 1   **DUNDEE UNITED** 0
Huistra (71 mins)

THE RANGERS team that took to the field this day, had an unfamiliar look to it. Missing for one reason or another were Stevens, Steven, McCall, McCoist and Hateley. It was going to be a special day regardless – a day in which nearly 43,000 ecstatic fans would hail the Champions as Richard Gough was presented with the League Trophy at the end of the match.

Of the game itself, both Andy Goram and John Brown were once again immense and kept United at bay. The decisive moment came in 71 minutes when a Pieter Huistra strike was deflected over Alan Main by defender John Clark.

It was the Dutchman's seventh goal of the season (his most memorable certainly being that superb equaliser against Bruges in Belgium in the European Cup) and was enough to secure victory.

Certainly of more than just passing interest was the fact that this final home result ensured that Rangers' league statistics for the season at Ibrox would read 20 victories and only 2 drawn games. Not a defeat in sight!

The European Cup beckoned once again for Rangers. It would be difficult to surpass the glories of this season but maybe.... ∎

RANGERS: Goram, Kuznetsov, D. Robertson, Gough (Murray), McPherson, Brown, Hagen (Mikhailitchenko), Ferguson, McSwegan, Durrant, Huistra.

CHAMPIONS

'Super' and 'Bomber' celebrate after Pieter Huistra (below) has clinched the final 1992/93 league match with this strike.

RICHARD THE

THE PRIDE was there for all to see as Richard Gough raised the Scottish Cup high in the air. It was a moment of great pleasure for the Club Captain in particular as the 'Bears' celebrated in style at Parkhead.

Once again, Gough had combined his remarkable leadership qualities with that will of iron, to produce an inspirational performance and in doing so, lead Rangers to their first domestic 'Treble' in fifteen years.

It had been a frustrating stop-go season for Richard but now that was all in the past. Earlier in the year, he had notched up his 200th competitive appearence for Rangers – an impressive tally achieved in less than five seasons with the club.

There have been many unforgettable occasions along the way .....the famous equaliser against Celtic in the dying seconds of the October 1987 game (when Rangers were reduced to nine men, with Graham Roberts in goal in place of the dismissed Chris Woods) .....his first final as a Rangers Captain, in which he scored the winner of the 2-1 Skol Cup victory over Celtic. Magical memories, indeed.

The lion-hearted Gough stands proud as a truly great Ranger. Of that, there can be no doubt. ■

Opposite: A triumphant pose from a truly courageous Rangers Captain.

LIONHEART

Season 1992/93
FUN QUIZ

1. Can you name the scorers of Rangers' first and last goals of the season?

2. Who did Rangers defeat in the final of the Glasgow Cup?
   The score and scorer(s) please.

3. How many games did The Light Blues play in the season?

4. Rangers scored five goals on four separate occasions. Name their opponents.

5. Rangers' biggest home crowd of the season totalled more than 46,000 fans.
   True or False?

6. Before this year's epic 'Battle of Britain' encounter, Rangers had played
   Leeds United in the Fairs Cup Quarter-final in 1968. What were the respective
   Ibrox and Elland Road leg scores?

7. Who was Rangers' top scorer against Celtic in the year?

8. How many 'Hat-tricks' did both Ally and Mark achieve in the season?

9. Give Rangers' winning scores at Parkhead.

10. Re-arrange the following words into a well known phrase:
    WHITE ARMY BLUE SMITH'S WALTER AND

Answers on Page 64

ANSWERS

Photo-Fun Quiz

1. Manager, Walter Smith.   2. 'Super' Ally McCoist.
3. Undefeated World Middleweight Champion, Chris Eubank.

1992/93 Fun Quiz

1. Ally McCoist; Mark Hateley.
2. Celtic, 1–0. Scorer, Charlie Miller.
3. A staggering 64 matches!
4. Dumbarton & Stranraer (Skol Cup); St. Johnstone & Falkirk (Premier League).
5. True – 2nd January, 1993, v Celtic (46,039).
6. Ibrox, 0–0. Elland Road, Leeds 2 Rangers 0.
7. Ian Durrant, with 2 goals.
8. Ally 5, Mark 0.
9. 1–0 (v Celtic); 2–1 (v Hearts); 2–1 (v Aberdeen).
10. ! ! ! Did you really have to look this one up?

ACKNOWLEDGEMENTS

Designed by Douglas Russell and John Traynor, with special assistance from Lisa Russell.

Typesetting and Origination by Inglis Allen, Kirkcaldy.

Bound in Scotland by Hunter & Foulis, Edinburgh.

All photographs supplied by *The Sun*.

Every effort has been made by the publishers to ensure the accuracy of all details and information in this publication.

Printed and Published in Scotland by

INGLIS ALLEN

40 Townsend Place, Kirkcaldy, Fife, Scotland KY1 1HF.
ISBN 0-9519694-4-7 © Inglis Allen 1993. All rights reserved.